T0151838

The Porcupinity of the Stars

Gary Barwin

COACH HOUSE BOOKS | TORONTO

first edition

Published with the generous assistance of the Canada Council for
the Arts and the Ontario Arts Council. Coach House Books also
acknowledges the Government of Ontario through the Ontario Book
Publishing Tax Credit and the Government of Canada through the
Canada Book Fund.

LIBRARY AND ARCHIVES CANADA CATALOGUING IN PUBLICATION

Barwin, Gary
The Porcupinity of the Stars / Gary Barwin

ISBN 978-1-55245-235-6

I. Title.

PS8553.A783P67 2010   C811'.54   C2010-903886-X

do why worry we?
word every earth on is
in place perfect the

ONE

PLANTING CONSENT

I carried my TV down the stairs
buried it on a hill
with a beautiful view

by spring a small antenna
sprouted in that place

somewhere under the earth
wispy clouds and the wingbeats of birds

INSIDE H

it is dark and soft
the world is a towel

a little priest raises his arms
he will speak with an open mouth
a glimpse of the planet
its fleshy inner core

plush H towel people
we mist the sky with our blue plum lungs
make heaven heron-dark with our breathing
fog the limits with spirit and blue exhalation

in each of us
lungs that are H
for we belong to the air

h
I say
H
because it is a pleasure and a surprise to breathe

FEET

I cut off my left, give it to the sea
others give their right

father, sister, mother, shoes
I look out at the ocean

heart, kidneys, lungs, brother
I wait for the consolation of water

OPPOSABLE CONSCIOUSNESS

under the papers of my desk
I discover
a small stone

yesterday I invented fire
today
I will create
a new tool
I will call it hammer

I pick up the stone
I smash it against my forehead

the clouds part and there is thunder
the trumpets of my ears
signal those to the east of me
those to the west
an army sets out across a blood red sea

a tiny baby is propped
in wet sand between the shores
I will call it baby
a useful tool
neither one thing
nor the other

shaman of the wallpaper
headboard priest in boxers
we wander the glad morning
where the sighing future waits

a sweet flower surrounds us
our fingers the dark plough of anxious hours
sun falls on the melismatic bones of heroes
each cup of clever sky clinging to
the city like a snowflake in the mouth

this is the earth
fences more tolerable than dreams
jockey shorts in the jaws of
each well-formed heart in every pleasant land

dancing on the road I feel
oxen fall from my shoulders
mother, children, father
wading away from night

there's a seraph on my bosom
fate on apathy's glimmering brow
lips are blue fire lashes
or idle thought

an hour an eye I love
earth's contingent language
ancient blue petal

SOME OF THE PARTS

the girl pushed
a long-handled broom
along the floor
Father could hardly bear it
tears streamed from his eyes
silent laughter transformed his face
his body was shaken with
spasms of delight

he was a bird
no bigger than a dust mite
looking for his place
in the world

his lifted wings were
invisible to all who knew
the broom as broom

the pleasurable eddies
of the Big Bang
the broad sweep
of time across the floor
the updraft of memory

those who knew
felt the swoop
of Father's wings
saw them raised in quaking splendour as
he created from the spasms
of his tiny body
the rippling laughter
the swept-clean ghost

ONE-FACED

don't do it, I said
choosing a piece of toast
a perfect fried egg

but she unhooked her jaw
and swallowed the sun

now it was really dark
and she stood up from the table
breakfast was over

I couldn't find my running shoes
or my briefcase hand
my dreams were of the moon spitting
as I tried to play chess

my abdomen was a sand dune
shaped by the wind
into the grains of a million
directionless games of beach volleyball

an infinite number of piglets
gnawed on my fingers, which were sprouting
uncomfortably from every orifice
there was no coffee

the paperboy crawled up the stairs
then ran away
bakers made bread but the yeast didn't care
and nothing rose

the day passed

my wife called friends
arranged a carnival
crocheted a thunderstorm while I slept

she made lunch in darkness
used the bones of the dog to retread
the parson's tires

and the sun
a hero with but one vast and burning face
travelled all day
through the sparkling labyrinth of my wife

when it was time
she lay on the lawn
and the sprinkler kicked in

we watched a brass band founded by groundhogs
overturn glasses of milk
birds flew from our mailbox
and her friends gathered round

don't do it, I said in my sleep
it'll be the end of you, I said

but my wife was already writhing
making divots in the sod
her left leg thrashed
then split the picnic table in two

fast-food wrappers filled the sky
and the swimsuits of the ancients
released their chlorine

I woke from my thousand-year slumber to see
the sun
born from the womb of my wife

daylight returning
blinkless and new

OPTICS, METEOROLOGY AND GEOMETRY

I accept nothing
as true

I carry my thoughts
a long way

I consider the difficulties
I leave nothing out

unless it
recognizes me

I avoid the rain
I try to love the snow's blank stare

STAY HERE WARPED HYPOTHESIS

I must remember to dismember
the moribund hopscotch of my guffaw
my cortical scrabble
the angelic bread-breeder wisdom
that clouds the knees

Was there ever a time when
the mailbox was corpulent with spent fish
my tongue a horror of patchwork facemask bosons
stalemate boomerang fortitude clogging my arms?

But I expect you've heard about
the moving elbows of my attempts to multiply
my skin set upon a mast
and the shapely blade of water
creasing my cow-friendly
chest hairs in the crepuscular zither

Ride with me in the woodblock
a premonition of slack
and a thousand birds buffeting
torrents of my eye-bleached ballet

Let me speak plainly:
in the creaking corner
a toolbox sorrow and the tonsils
a reply of desk bus overalls and
a tithe on the ledge of before-I-was-born

I run
I satiate
I porous gratitude in the rust-bound palaver
you are a shrewd arithmetic of mention
the recanted pyjamas of scent

Mention me
O statutory gasp of the nosedive
Together, we are a nebula on the precipice of sport

THEORY OF FALLACIES

Howie out with the hose again
someone singing opera from the above-ground pool
in their backyard the grim brothers undressing
wolf-as-granny
moon hangs low over the neighbourhood
tries to catch a peek

❧

ants gather around the barbecue tongs
gasoline rainbows on the tarmac
a seven-year-old tries to run along the curb
man with the face of a pelican
squeezes out greatness
late in the afternoon

❧

inside the deck chair
night thick as a thrush
birds hover
girl's hair in their beaks
a crown of birds above her
and she sighs

❧

a gecko climbs my spine
the front steps to my holiday home
welcome, Maria the maid says
everything is ready for you
to live forever
memory folded back
every night before bed

≈

there are five men in black suits
chasing me
I'm wearing a duck mask
someone else's spotted underwear

I have never found
a useful philosophy

≈

next door
he had one wing
shut like a huge blind eye
and Jimmy, oh
little Jimmy
loved the atoms like pets

≈

my brother and I fill the bath with ducks
their yellow bobbing like Father's eyes
staring out from his big chair
we're on our knees leaning over the edge
arms wet with soapy water
a procession of swirling ducks

we look into each other's eyes
large wings spurt from our backs
reach to the cracks of the ceiling
we are flightless as oceans
and the windows
are open

≈

the end of days
a chef on a cellphone
a single shoe on the road

Howie is down in the basement
musket ball between his teeth
his wounds are a hundred years old
and for sure he's late for dinner

≈

in the dark lapel
of my only suit
I place
a squirting flower
a grey flower squirting
night into your peaceful face

take that!
small grey remembered day

≈

it is almost night
the philosopher reads
Descartes through the body
of Rudolph
the Transparent Boy

breath slices light
to ribbons

HISTORY NOTEBOOK

'you're a know-nothing'
sky says to me

'sky's right'
ground says

I make it rain
I boil the trees
and the giraffes
loud as knives

I raise babies
pink between the slats of cribs
I make boats run through the sea
I make the boll weevils cry

I'm a know-nothing baby
stuck between
ground and sky

I put my foot in the river
and I move on

EVERTHELESS

I laugh whether or not the gobsmacked laugh –
me with the snorting face and short memory –
I laugh whether the foxes, which began so soberly
ended snuffling and begging
and I laugh myself
whether or not the blind beer-garden apes were proud to be judges
or whether the cowardly midwinter boys made
me bedridden with poison-soaked weapons
because if luck filters pretty things
and fate gives us broken hands
to hinge and squeal and kiss
and if the heart in the body is
torn up, tore up, cut and restocked
still the beautiful laughter remains
dusky and firefly
left with the ashes

PSALM

By the late-night pickup window, we sat and wept
when we remembered ourselves

We hung our TVs upon the air in the midst thereof

For there our captors required of us songs
they that seized us, required of us joy
saying, 'Sing us one of the songs of Keith'

How shall we sing Danny's song in a strange land?

If I forget thee, O Chris and freedom
may my right hand forget how to make dog shadows by lamplight

If I do not remember thee, Tracy and peacetime
may my tongue cling to the roof of the bus as it goes on tour
if I prefer not Laurie and justice above my chief joy

Remember, O Keith, what Carol and Mike did
in the days of fire
who said, 'Tear them down. Tear them down. Tear them down!'

O de facto American children, doomed to destruction,
happy is he who repays you

He who taketh and dasheth your babies
against the screen

FISH

1

fish school beneath
the skin of lake

I am a small boy
calling

a bridge between fish
and voice

there is a path between blood
and lake

2

two trees fight with axes
a third wears a mask

in the branches
a sparrow hawk chases a rat

water is blindfolded
you throw a knife at it

3

on my shoulders
the head of a youth

marry me, the water says
lifts its veil

mouths become waves

THE ORIGINAL MIDDLE

I was born with my head
in the middle of nowhere

until someone placed a rock on it
then I knew

where I was

which rock
I was under

so when I learned to walk
I walked

always
in the cool shade

O

My daughter gave me Ireland
I put it in my pocket

out of my other pocket I gave her France

O things with shape and no shape
keep it up!

TWO

GLACIER

I wake and switch on the bedside light
there's a glacier in my bed
ice, it says
snow, it says
it turns and presses its cold mouth on mine
the frigid slurry and recession
the mile-thick compression
the scraping out of lakes and the flattening of mountains
I have been waiting for you, it says

REGRET

there is a lake
and the wind
unsettled

what is it we hope for?
ourselves out here on the peninsula

a path through the trees
where there is no path

a stand of trees where
there is no standing

egret

heron

our own footprints in the sand ahead
before the tide moves in

FOURTEEN BEAUTIFUL DOGS

the field beside my heart is
filled with ugly deer and one beautiful dog

a poem doesn't have to have fourteen perfect lines
or else you're spitting on graves

maybe you'll slip up and tell a truth
stick your elbow into something

under the moon your tongue hangs out
you'd like to howl but

the horizon grows ever larger
please save my family from complication or sudden death

listen: a small movement in the linden leaves
be brave be brave be brave

and here's another beautiful dog
sighing sighing sighing

INVERTING THE DEER

I

the deer of this earth are doubly inverted
once, and their antlers point toward the centre

(the antlers of inverted deer point toward
the antlers of every other inverted deer)

once again, and their antlers point toward space

2

do not touch deer
and you will not touch deer

do not walk on deer
and you will not walk on deer

do not mourn deer when you are dying
though their noses are against the glass

do not mourn deer when you are dying
though their minds are edgeless

3

fish swim around the remembered hooves of deer
they understand
they know

4

antlers grow toward
the deer which grow toward the ground

the wind rustles the hair of deer
the deer are a harp

5

when the first trees
whose home was the water
whose home was the sky
began to die
the deer did not know what to do

and so, their smooth heads wrinkling
their hooves beating the water
their hooves beating the air
they ran through the world weeping

until they planted the branches
and crossed the world
trees growing like memories
from the tops of old televisions
from the tops of old brown heads

6

there is only one deer
and it is larger than sky

the deer has but one season
and the hunters wait for it
after a great while
the hunters become trees
and bullets lose their green

night falls in the skyless rivers
and deer's breath warns the sky

RELIEVING

Daddy said
Son you have to make your own dog
if you have none

and I said
I have a fire hydrant
so I can just imagine

A ROOF FLOORED

the stone hopes for flight
the way a goose
wants power chords

you either treasure the shine
or sneeze in the shrine

stuffed with documents and crickets
daylight awards the huffing
of the beautiful and numinous
to the furthest crow

yes: we are the roof and the roof and the roof
we sit before the mirror
use night as ballast

HEINRICH MANOEUVRES

1

bald head in the high north
covered with a doily of snow

dreams its body
flickering and mouthless
a burning wall

the fragile crown between
this life and the next

2

dawn sputters over the mountain
and in the distance, a flock of sheep rings
my sweetheart, my lamb, my son
I speak these things gladly

helicopters, oncology, a rain of darts
no curtain moves:
he lies still, maybe
dreams

3 BROKEN GATE

don't leave with hands
glued like prayer or a cave
the whip upon my face
believing I were a cliff

let it not be in vain
don't leave with these tortures
hectoring my chilblains
my tonsils, testicles

I waited
but you did not come
went mad as the cage
round my bones

for waiting breaks
day over its pointed tongue
I drove each instant up a ladder
two rungs up
one down: I sank back
but you said nothing

O lottery of flowers
how I believe
the broken gate

a child king
with wet, pale cheeks.
we sat under the green
limited-access highway
and closed our little briefcases
the child presented me with a memo:

'I does not want my father to be a throne
I does not want his demanding croon
his Sinatra howl
throwing me over the mountains

'I wants to be a shadow only
one that cannot be
that speaks as I lies in the grave
only when I becomes night
will I be clear'

5

into the hands of the piano
I pour my right arm

full of boughs
mouth deeply fresh fallen

our wide world
the cavernous tree

6

glowing red-sun stogies
rosy angel horks
boiling-up water
luring the shoreline
waking the shy dust

a wax mask
breaks from the moon
the glamour of stars
small, bald
innocent

its lone splendour
the soft moths of its husbands
still beautiful

INBOGGANING

a jacket has three sleeves so we have three arms

&

when it's time for dinner, the sun sets

&

if you move slowly enough, you are lapped by the forest

&

they close their eyes on the hilltop. they inboggan

&

the deafness of snow, the blindness of fire, the tastelessness of sleep

&

trees never reach their destination, except to begin again

&

no two snowflakes or fingerprints the same; identical days

&

there is something tornadoesque about the distance,
the horizon like wood grain, or a hairstyle

&

everything is backward; even when it's backward

❧

for show and tell, the ocean brought the boy to school

❧

everysome is elsecome thing

FIDO

the horizon darkening
a semaphore man drops his flags
opens his lunchbox
has a thermos of tea
and a white sandwich

when he is done
he picks up his flags
holds out his arms
and waits

the road, ever faithful
waits with him

ON LISTENING TO COLEMAN HAWKINS

some think our ears
radiant fetuses

driving their tiny cars
on either side of the head

how do we know magnificence?

the disco ball of the heart
a mosaic of shiny blood
that's there and then not

SHOPPING FOR DEER

I went shopping for deer
there were no deer
the shopping cart became the deer

I brought it home
climbed inside
and turned off the lights

the seasons changed
I lived on earth
sometimes the bright sun shone
I became old

when I die, I will remember the deer
I will remember its wheels and antlers
I will remember its flesh and lightning
its womb of silver bones

THE PROBLEM OF BREATH IN OUR AGE

the other months are clean
so I'm vacuuming August
dusting away the remnants of summer
the invoice for light that the sun sent
expecting the horizon to pay for the days' sparkle

there's a fawn up the flagpole here at Camp Bambi
it's unflappable
though the wandering abacuses count their teeth lucky
in love with stationery, staplers and my desk chair
how to report this to Accounting
accurately and without alerting the campers
or the piles of rubble, elected by a landslide?

Oh, there is no darkness under the floorboards
or anywhere else, really
light wears its brittle nightgown
its soft body a chrysalis for dusk
it's more of a mood that fills the world with night

GRIEF

I dig a hole in the grass
my son takes the spade

digs the hole deeper
big enough for his sister

then she makes the hole
big enough for him

we gather around
unsure of what to say

the hole says nothing
it listens

ARCHIVIST OF THE FUTURE

other people have desires
I have a piano falling in my ear

old testament jazz and the piano sheds its wings

it fell from the long-fingered tree
its broken spine lines the street
its many windows cross
the dust-coloured mind
the intimate power of salt and smoke and scotch
painful as a book

let them have desires, I say
I have a piano
and music's inconceivable bruise
in my ear

In the city of voices, she throws her voice
and the multitudinous ears of the crowd catch.

Wisdom she preaches by the gates of reproach,
and in the city of sayings, she says:

I pour my spirit over you and, wearing no coat, you must listen.
I use words to make my words known,
stretch out my hands but you clasp not my tongue.

When will the scorners cease their scorning,
the faces of fools face facts?

My jeers sit astride your calamities like a hurricane,
and as a jockey I deride your fear.

Like home invaders, adversity and distress burst through the door,
then fear and calamity appear on the threshold
dressed up for Halloween.

I've snuffed the candle in the pumpkin,
turned the porch light dark.

Inside the broken ark of your brain,
knowledge is a blackbird braided by shadow
shredding the holy books to nest.

You've made your bed of salt,
now for every season there's a path through the brine.

Do not eat your own counsel only.
The simple slay themselves with their own advice,
a sword without edges, and are cleft by feathers.

Live in my voice, for whosoever hearkens to me
dwelleth confidently, and has flight without sky.

Be quiet from fear of evil.

SMALL APES AND WHITE FEET

moon drifts in cloud
I've half a mind
to borrow
a small ape

&

what does the man next door do
with his two perfect
feet?

&

the moon is following me
so am I

&

I will gaze at the moon
until it worries
about me

&

the snap of a butterfly
a book
beneath my feet

&

a pleasant crackling of bones
as I walk
pursued by no one

*

since my house burned down
I plug the television
into the ground

*

what does the man next door do
with one perfect
foot?

FURNACE COAT

on the forty-second floor
the comptroller
sits with
a blowtorch
melting windows
and the memo on his desk

my life is
a single burning
ice cube
dropped into punch
splashes my little yard of space-time
ashes
over my asbestos body

I have lungs like
desert islands
on one of them
a guy wearing an inner tube
praying to be saved

on the other
a different guy in an inner tube
praying to the first

on the soundtrack
I am singing

I have matches
here
let me light
your birthday candles

oh look!
here's my life
its little cover says
'You too can go to College'
but of course I can't
because
I just went

I was an ant farm
a pickle trainer
a philosophy-of-clowning auditor

my resume
a maraschino cherry that
fits on my nose
is covered with ants
smoke fills the room

breathe
the instructors say
sit down and
breathe

GUN LIPS

.the river is a gun
the mountain is a gun
the sun sets inside the bullet wound
red and safe

sister of the gun

there are directions the fingers don't point
this feeling: landing, breathing
landing and breathing

gravity thinks about the mountain
licking its gun lips
its shadow hands

eventually, grinning
everything falls

THREE

WHATEVER-IT-WAS

a casket of weeping birds
the old kindness

last ship of the ancient dead
whiplash from a bell

the moon does not recall
whatever-it-was

the sleepy ground
called only the mind

pale blossom behind the eyelids

everywhere should whisper
in our footsteps

BRICK

I will take care of the brick
because it came through my window

it is a damaged bird
unable to fly

I will make a safe bed for it
as I would help any broken thing

the truncated dove of a hand
the message that told me run

FOURTH PERSON

FIRST PERSON

the person with the breasts
the very long toenails
the yellow nose

then another one with breasts
no arms
a toenail taller than a tree

it's supposed to be a toenail but
in real life it's
a balcony

see how it has
a mouth
a fancy mouth

and a nose and ears
now I need to make
a body

this body is
pregnant
see the baby?

and the vagina
and now
I have to make
a sun

actually it doesn't need a sun
that's the lady's hat

she's just planning
to go outside

she doesn't know that
this picture is warm

SECOND PERSON

this guy is mean
he doesn't like
people
and he has rosy cheeks

but he's still a kid
he's got three nipples because
he's mad
that makes his two nipples turn into
three

his vagina
wait! he's not a boy
his bum
his pet cat

here's his sad cat
the cat's hair
like the colour of the cat

THIRD PERSON

this guy is grown up
he's a captain and he's lost his
eye

he's a boy so he has
nipples

his forehead
his mouth
his hair
this is his dog and
this is his penis
these are Niagara Falls
and this is the guy

his chair
his neck
his hair
his feet
and Niagara Falls

he's looking at Niagara Falls
and he's pretty mad
because they're all above him and
some are coming down

FOURTH PERSON

this guy's unhappy
and he's a bird
a Chinese bird
with a hat on him
but he doesn't know

he's a boy

nipple
nipple

and he's very fancy

wings
wings

and he's flying

WE ARE FAMILY

an organism which presses
against the planet

an organism which has hair
(sad, believable hair)
that refuses to believe

which has sensations
sick moves
and an interesting history

an organism which holds up its fingers
how many fingers
(if fingers are what they are)?

an organism with other organisms on it
and upon which it rains

an organism which sleeps
soft as a cloth

a baby in a bed full of babies
and the earth full of babies

THE LOOKOUT MAN

1

the woman is a high school calculus teacher
she knows nothing about synchronized swimming
she is in love

two brothers
a brother and a sister
a man and a woman
one of them balding

bummer!

2

if you are in love, wear light shoes

if you are sad and have an interest in automobiles
wear black shoes

but shh!
the secret rendezvous

3

the woman thinks of something frying
eyebrows on a griddle
shoes on an alien planet
a miniaturized love machine

you must understand synchronized swimming
to be lookout man

4

a white shoe denotes sorrow
the moral high ground

automobiles have trouble on high ground

driver
wear one white shoe

like your passenger
your other foot will be a shadow

keep it on the brake

5

when observed from a great distance
they are lovers

say goodbye to the stop sign

they understand that
ears give little joy

6

those who have a shadow or are depicted as dark
treasure their inner light

the shadow of a curb is sentient

hey! somebody forgot to colour in the sidewalk

7

specks or small globs of calculus
dropping from the sky

many years later
they meet again in a restaurant

the one with the most fulfilling life
tells the worst jokes

AUBADE

we wake together
put on the same
oversized skin

it's baggy and there's
room for both of us inside
I shave while you
wash where required

we choose clothes
our favourite belt and shoes
share breakfast
open the door to the bone-blue world

much larger and brighter
pinker than yesterday

THE WINDPIPE OF SLEEP

the split joint of sleep
a slice of meat against the grain

ↄ

Tell them they have nothing to worry about. Hold two pencils vertically in front of their eyes.

ↄ

When the glistening arachnoid layer covering the exterior of the pia mater. When its glistening inner surface.

both nerve and cloud
the cerebellum
a stump of optic nerve

ↄ

Turn a frog on its back. Carefully expose the origins of the nearest spiral galaxy. Ask an eight-year-old boy about the night sky. Place a finger of his right hand into warm water (a finger of his right eye into water). Observe the hand of your companion in a uniformly lighted state such as Ontario. What is the distance at which the hand disappears?

Sit facing a window. Quickly uncover a small blue Renault.

Prepare a frog by destroying its brain as soon as it is under the influence of ether. Note the reaction of frog, 1) when toe is pinched, 2) when, attended by a poet, it dives into a stagnant pool.

   nerves to eyes
   nerves to nose
   blotting paper, some stout scissors

Count a boy's pulse and breathing while he is sitting quietly. Let him run a hundred yards at full speed. Tickle the inside of his nose with a feather. There is a live frog on his bedroom wall.

The casing of the brain split open, the starlight flowing from the belly of the muscle breaking into finer and finer branches, becoming too small to be followed without the aid of a microscope. There is present abundant energy to construct the walls, floors, the roof of mouth.

A knock at the door. A man walks in. A bone forceps, some blunt wire, a signal may be passed from one hand to another.

   raise the brain in front
   you raise the brain

≈

Attach a large tube to a nozzle. Space for the heart. The lobes. On a first date, a lung.

≈

Cut open a blood clot. Your mouth, a thermometer weeping. A mirror or knife blade. You burn yourself shaving in a wide-mouthed jar.

≈

the nervous system of Herman Melville
a Finnish haiku
the windpipe of sheep

≈

At the moment of breath, you use your hands to be an owl.

AFTER BINYON

I shall not grow old
as the part of me that's left
grows old
rage shall not weary me
nor the damn years

yes, and at the sunset
in the morning
and all afternoon
and for much of the night
I'll remember me

HORSE

somewhere
in the far north

of Toronto
my son and I destroy

a shipping crate containing
a wooden horse

we put the horse
and bits of smashed crate

into the car and
drive home

we put the horse
in the yard

that night
no one climbs out of
my son

REALISM

run into a brick wall

if you believe
you can go through

bones ring like a bell

THREE TREATISES

infancy
teams up with the heart

or something

later:
something else

SONG

a happy man flying with jet shoes
t's emanating from his ears
t t t t t t t t t t t all through the sky
and onto the blood-red bus

a beautiful sight
we stared at it for the rest of the night

TWO SONGS

1
little human songbook
cloud face
I is that turns in song
my every am
bent

2
morning

glad I star-steal

with care

POEM

patience
we're enjoying
leaflessness

FROST

two roads diverged in a yellow wood
I took one
it doesn't matter which

I'm not giving it back

AUTUMN IN THE TOOLBOX

blam!
a leaf falls

a hammer repeats
what we already know

SHOUT

'day,' a man shouts
'night,' shouts another
they continue until they are old

neither dark nor light
day nor night

SUNDAYS AT THE MUSEUM

a long hall fenced by teeth

'I ...' begins Marta the cleaning lady, leaning on her mop

THE SKY IS NO REASON

two children with identical faces
ride an ostrich

we are not afraid
of anything
they say

well maybe our mother
if we're not clean

there was the black dog
but now
we are dressed in the black dog
headpieces
ride the black feathers
on the rounded rump
the useless wings
of the ostrich

the sky is completely
empty now
so no reason to fly
no reason
to be
afraid

❧

[from *Physiologus*]

the ostrich
flies low over the face of the earth
visits the blacksmith
devours red-hot iron
passes it immediately through its intestine
it emerges glowing
lightened and purified

the ostrich lays eggs but
does not brood in the usual way:
it stares intensely
they grow warm in the heat of its gaze
and its young are hatched

&

later, the ostrich farmer's son plumps
his pillow during sleep
a man dressed in black
walks a field

a stone thrown out a trailer window

under the moon,
cracks in an egg

ears of corn flinch
somewhere on the screen
snow falls with a hiss

inside the head
egg is moon
the head also egg
ostrich in its shell

speaking with snowfall
at the back of the mind
corn fear
in the eyes
also
stalks of fingers

the corn man is stone
heavy breathing
obsidian
wading the white noise of feathers

‌～

if I could choose
a face
I would choose the face
of the ostrich rider

laconic
as an asterisk
or a patient star
iridescent and expressionless
a black dog in the wrinkled sky

I would choose the face
of the ostrich rider
for my second face also

I do not want
to be
afraid or
red hot

I do not want to be
afraid

SONG

Everybody cheering! Happy!
And start to eat.
Excited.
The boy drops a glass.
So unexpectable.
Screaming opens widely its mouth.
A small fire starts. Very fast.

They take it like real.
He is artificial lake.
and the storm sings.
Now they are staying on the distance
and watch.
Watch!

HOSE

my son left the hose on all night
snails inched across the sidewalk

not knowing the pool was filled with water
not knowing that water had filled the pool

my son left the hose on all night
glass slid through the snake like jewels

COMEDY

go to sleep
then get up again

be crucified
then rise

eat a bomb, sure
but meet your sweetie for dinner

I let the dragon into the house
and it burns both piano and shoes

our home is an ashen cloud with an incomprehensible address
barefoot, we walk to the store for ice cream

slip on a moose

MY GRANDFATHER

had no time for
description

he said
I'm too old

at my age
I just want to know

what happens

SMALL SUPPER

1

we placed our shadows inside birds
where they can't be found

shadows in birds nesting between the shadowy hands of trees
or flocking across the blue-lit sky

shadows cast only
when beaks are open

2

it was then
we put our shadows there
or the potential for shadows

the shadow of a shadow
is my friend

and my friend's shadow
is nighttime in the shape of a friend

3

the creature that rises then bends toward the earth
is a bird

a mountain can't fly unless
the ground disappears

4

a thousand darknesses in the chests of small birds
barely visible from the earth
a pupil in the centre of an iris
not dark but transparent
absorbing almost all light

5

it's not so much that Polly wants a cracker
but that the lark wants its small supper of sky
its late dinner of twilight among the blue leaves

6

now a bird's small shadow is in my chest
the branches of the ribs
the chest-blue sky

THE PORCUPINITY OF THE STARS

I scoop out the inside of my face
spit the seeds
at the Welcome Wagon

children, enter my empty head
I have dangerous zits and a porcupine
also a hammock of great ideas

some kind of emotion whirrs like cards
stuck between the spokes of my teeth
or the library

they ask me
what will we see
through your one blind eye?

and I say, the childless stars which spangle
the dark thong of the faceless sky
the pole-dancing god who made me

ALPHABET

his river-like face

has taken my face
my river face

brother, sister, future, past
between the right eye and the left

the mouth speaks

ACKNOWLEDGEMENTS

Porcupinity is for my family.

Some of these poems first appeared in the following anthologies:

Surreal Estate, ed. Stuart Ross (The Mercury Press); poem, home, eds. Jenny Hill and Dan Waber (Paper Kite Press); ditch, anthology 1: Canadian Innovative Poets, ed. J. Goodman (ditchpoetry.com); 25 Years of Tree, eds. J. Moran and J. Mulligan (BuschekBooks);

and in the following magazines, journals and small presses:

dig, filling station, NationalPoetryMonth.ca, Writing Space Journal, draft, above/ground press, Musicworks, curved h&z , Taddle Creek, Hammered Out, Spire, Vallum, Peter F. Yacht Club, Raw Nervz, Precipice.

Several of these poems appeared in the chapbook Inverting the Deer (serif of nottingham) which was a co-winner of the 2009 bpNichol Chapbook Award.

Thanks to the editors and readers of all those publications for first considering them.

'Evertheless' is after a sonnet by Heine.
'Some of the Parts': the first stanza is adapted from 'Birds' in
      The Street of Crocodiles by Bruno Schulz.
'A Floor Roofed' is after a poem by Rilke.
'Planting Consent' is for David W. McFadden.
'Inside H' is, of course, for bpNichol.
'Optics, Meteorology and Geometry' and 'Theory of Fallacies'
      are after Descartes.
'O' is for Gabriel Gudding.

'Inverting the Deer' is for Craig Conley.

'History Notebook' is for Kerry Schooley.

'Heinrich Manouevers' is after poems by Heine.

'Fourth Person' is for my daughter, Rudi.

'My Grandfather' is for Percy Zelikow.

'The Lookout Man' is after *The Lovers*, a painting by Philip Surrey.

'The Sky Is No Reason: Physiologus' is adapted from the
     'Ostrich' entry in *The Wordsworth Dictionary of Symbolism*.

'The Problem of Breath in Our Age' is after James Tate and
     Kevin Connolly.

'Archivist of the Future' is adapted from *The Archivist* by
     Martha Cooley.

'Small Apes and White Feet' is after haiku by Basho, Massahide,
     Zeami and Shiki.

Some of these poems were written with the assistance of the
Kurzweil Cybernetic Poet software. Most used old-school English
language technology.

Thanks also to the supporters of public funding for the arts
for your help in the writing, publishing, presentation and
promotion of these works as well as the vibrant context within
which they exist.

Writing and writers exist in a community. Thanks to my friends
and writing colleagues including Ryan Barwin, Gregory Betts,
derek beaulieu, Craig Conley, Geof Huth, members of Meet the
Presses, Stuart Ross, Kerry Schooley and Hugh Thomas, and to the
people at Coach House including Alana Wilcox, Evan Munday, Stan
Bevington, Christina Palassio and Kira Dreimanis. I'd especially
like to thank Kevin Connolly for his encouraging, intelligent,
perceptive and incisive editing. Maybe I could slip in some of the
deleted bits here ...

GARY BARWIN is a poet, fiction writer, composer and performer. His music and writing have been performed and broadcast in Canada, the U.S. and Europe. His publications include poetry: *Outside the Hat* and *Raising Eyebrows* (Coach House), *Servants of Dust* (No Press), *anus porcupine eyebrow* (Supernova Tadpole/Paper Kite) and *frogments from the frag pool*  (with derek beaulieu) (The Mercury Press); and fiction: *DoctorWeep and other Strange Teeth*, *Big Red Baby* and *The Mud Game* (a novel with Stuart Ross) (The Mercury Press). Forthcoming books include *The Obvious Flap* (with Gregory Betts) (BookThug) and *Kafka Franzlations: A Guide to the Imaginary Parables* (with Hugh Thomas and Craig Conley) (New Star). He was the co-winner of the 2009 bpNichol chapbook award for *Inverting the Deer* (serif of nottingham) and was a recipient of the K. M. Hunter Foundation Artist award. He edits supernova tadpole editions for Paper Kite Press. Barwin is also the author of several books for kids, including *Seeing Stars*, which was nominated for a CLA YA Book of the Year and an Arthur Ellis Award. Barwin received a PhD in Music Composition from SUNY at Buffalo. He lives in Hamilton, Ontario, with his wife and three children, and online at garybarwin.com. If you were the last word in this bio, you'd be home.

Typeset in Joanna
Printed and bound at the Coach House on bpNichol Lane, 2010
Edited for the press by Kevin Connolly
Designed by Evan Munday
Cover illustration by Charmaine Olivia
Author photo by Gary Barwin

Coach House Books
80 bpNichol Lane
Toronto Ontario M5S 3J4

416 979 2217
800 367 6360

mail@chbooks.com
www.chbooks.com